THE WORLD'S GREATEST
SPACE VEHICLES

Ian Graham

Raintree

www.raintreepublishers.co.uk
Visit our website to find out more information about Raintree books.

To order:
 Phone 44 (0) 1865 888112
Send a fax to 44 (0) 1865 314091
Visit the Raintree Bookshop at www.raintreepublishers.co.uk to browse our catalogue and order online.

First published in Great Britain by Raintree, Halley Court, Jordan Hill, Oxford, OX2 8EJ, part of Harcourt Education.
Raintree is a registered trademark of Harcourt Education Ltd.

© Harcourt Education Ltd 2006
The moral right of the proprietor has been asserted.

Editorial: Andrew Farrow and Dan Nunn
Design: Ron Kamen and Philippa Baile
Picture Research: Hannah Taylor and Elaine Willis
Production: Duncan Gilbert

Originated by Dot Gradations Ltd.
Printed in China

The paper used to print this book comes from sustainable resources.

British Library Cataloguing in Publication Data
Graham, Ian, 1953-
  Space vehicles. – (The world's greatest)
  1. Space vehicles – Juvenile literature
  I. Title
  629.4'7
A full catalogue record for this book is available from the British Library.

Acknowledgements
The publishers would like to thank the following for permission to reproduce photographs:

Associated Press pp. **14**, **15 bottom**; Corbis pp. **5** (Roger Ressmeyer), **6** (Sygma), **7 bottom**, **10**, **11 bottom** (Reuters), **11 top** (Reuters/Sergei Karpukhin), **12**, **13 top**, **16 top** (Roger Ressmeyer), **16 bottom**, **17** (Reuters), **19** (Reuters), **21 bottom** (Reuters/NASA), **22**, **24**; NASA pp. **1** (SPEX), **4** (SPEX), **13 bottom**, **15 top**; Science Photo Library pp. **7 top** (NASA), **8** (European Space Agency), **9** (David Ducros), **20**, **21 top** (NASA), **23** (Detlev Van Ravenswaay).

Cover photograph of the US Space Shuttle *Discovery* taking off on 29 October 1998 reproduced with permission of Getty Images.

Every effort has been made to contact copyright holders of any material reproduced in this book. Any omissions will be rectified in subsequent printings if notice is given to the publishers.

Contents

Words appearing in the text in bold, **like this**, are explained in the Glossary.

Space vehicles

The first space vehicle went into space in 1957. Now, lots of spaceflights are made every year. Most spacecraft fly around the Earth, but some have been sent to the Moon and planets.

Getting off the ground

Space vehicles are launched by rockets. The biggest rockets are made from two or more pieces. These are called stages. When each stage has used up its fuel and isn't needed any more, it falls away from the space vehicle.

*This diagram shows a stage falling away from the main rocket as it blasts its way through the **atmosphere**.*

The rocket engines of the Space Shuttle power it into the sky on its way to space.

Fast fliers

Do you know how fast spacecraft fly? A spacecraft flying around the Earth travels at 28,000 kph (17,400 mph). That's about 30 times faster than a jet airliner! Some spacecraft fly even faster. When the Apollo 10 spacecraft came back to Earth from a flight around the Moon, it reached nearly 40,000 kph (25,000 mph).

*Unmanned **space probes** have been sent to all of the planets except Pluto, the furthest away.*

The world's greatest space mission

On 16 July 1969, three American **astronauts** climbed into an Apollo spacecraft. They were Neil Armstrong, Edwin "Buzz" Aldrin, and Michael Collins. Four days later, Armstrong and Aldrin became the first people to walk on the Moon.

Setting course for the Moon

The Apollo spacecraft was launched by a giant rocket called the Saturn V ("V" means "5"). The rocket put the spacecraft in **orbit** around the Earth. When the spacecraft had been checked to make sure that everything was working properly, the rocket was fired again. This sent the spacecraft on its way to the Moon.

All the Apollo space missions to the moon were launched by the Saturn V rocket. It never failed.

Apollo Moon-landing missions

Mission	Launched
Apollo 11	1969
Apollo 12	1969
Apollo 14	1971
Apollo 15	1971
Apollo 16	1972
Apollo 17	1972

There was also an Apollo 13 **mission**, but it wasn't able to land on the Moon because of an explosion in the spacecraft. The crew returned to Earth safely.

Lunar Excursion Module – this part landed on the Moon.

Command Module – this part returned to Earth.

Service Module

This is the 3rd stage of the Saturn V.

Landing on the Moon

When the Apollo spacecraft reached the Moon, it fired a rocket. This put it in orbit around the Moon. Two of the astronauts, Armstrong and Aldrin, then landed part of Apollo on the Moon. Armstrong became the first person ever to step onto another world. About 600 million people, a fifth of all the people on Earth, watched it on television.

*This drawing shows the three parts of the Apollo spacecraft – the **Command module**, the **Service Module**, and the **Lunar Excursion Module**. You can also see the third stage of the Saturn V rocket.*

Apollo 11 carried the first people all the way to the Moon.

The most powerful space rockets

Europe's Ariane 5 rocket is one of the most powerful rockets for launching satellites today. Ariane 5 can launch satellites weighing as much as seven or eight family cars to a great height above the Earth! The nose-cone at the top of the rocket can fit two large satellites inside. The satellites Ariane carries are also called its **payload**.

Ariane rockets are launched from a Spaceport in South America. Most of the space inside an Ariane 5 launch rocket is filled with fuel.

Lift-off!

A main rocket and two boosters launch Ariane 5 into the sky. The boosters provide most of the force needed to lift Ariane off the launch-pad. They work for just over two minutes. Then they fall away. The main rocket carries on for another seven minutes or so. Then this falls away and a small upper rocket takes over. It places the satellites in orbit around the Earth.

payload

upper stage rocket

main stage rocket

booster rocket

booster rocket

This diagram shows the main parts of the Ariane 5 rocket.

Heavy launcher

Russia's Proton rocket carries heavy payloads into a low orbit above the Earth. It launches satellites and parts of space stations. Proton rockets have been used since the 1960s.

Ariane 5

Height:	Up to 55.4 m/181 ft 9 in
Diameter:	5.4 m/17 ft 9 in
Lift-off weight:	Up to 750,000 kg/1,653,470 lb
Maximum payload:	16 tonnes/35,275 lb

HIGH FIVE

Ariane 5 is as tall as a 12-storey building.

The most successful manned space vehicle

Russian Soyuz spacecraft have been carrying people into space since 1967.

The Soyuz spacecraft

A Soyuz spacecraft has three main parts. The crew can live in two of them. The other part is full of fuel and instruments. The spacecraft has small rockets called **thrusters**. These are used to steer it in space. It also has **solar panels** to make electricity from sunlight.

solar panels

Descent Module

Orbital Module

docking port

Instrument Module

Cosmonauts live and work in the Soyuz spacecraft's Orbital and Descent Modules.

When the Soyuz spacecraft returns to Earth, it uses a parachute to slow down before landing.

Space ferries

A Soyuz spacecraft can link up with other spacecraft. A door in the end of the Soyuz spacecraft opens when the spacecraft are connected. The crew can go through the door into the other spacecraft.

Soyuz craft carried crews to the Russian Salyut and Mir space stations. Today, they carry crews to the International Space Station. At the end of a mission, a crew returns to Earth. They travel in part of the spacecraft called the Descent **Module**. A heat shield on the front end protects the crew inside.

A Soyuz spacecraft can carry a crew of one, two, or three.

Soyuz TMA spacecraft

Crew:	**Up to 3**
Length:	**7.0 m/23 ft**
Diameter:	**2.7 m/9 ft**
Span (across solar panels):	**10.7 m/35 ft 1 in**
Weight:	**7,220 kg/15,915 lb**

The most reused spacecraft

The US Space Shuttle was the first space vehicle that could be used again and again, like an airliner. Space Shuttles have made more than 100 spaceflights since 1981.

The spaceplane

The Space Shuttle has four main parts. The astronauts fly inside the Orbiter. This is a spaceplane about the same size as a small airliner. A huge fuel tank and two rockets help it to take off. After launch, the empty fuel tank and booster rockets fall away. The Orbiter carries on into space.

A Space Shuttle is launched into the sky by its engines and booster rockets.

Returning to Earth

The Orbiter is covered with special materials that protect it from heat. These are needed because the Orbiter heats up as it returns through the air to Earth. It gets so hot that it glows! The Orbiter then glides down to land on a runway at the Kennedy Space Center in Florida, in the United States.

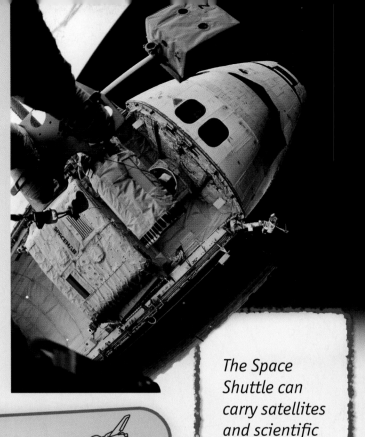

The Space Shuttle can carry satellites and scientific instruments in its cargo bay.

Space Shuttle Orbiter

Crew:	**2 pilots and up to 5 other astronauts**
Length:	**37.2 m/122 ft**
Wingspan:	**23.8 m/78 ft**
Weight:	**93,318 kg/218,960 lb**
Orbit height:	**Usually up to 400 km/248 miles above the Earth**

The commander of the Orbiter lands it on a runway like an airliner.

The biggest space station

Most manned spacecraft stay in space for a few weeks before they return to Earth. Space stations stay in space for years.

The biggest space station is being built now. It is called the International Space Station, or ISS, because several countries are helping to build it. It is so big that it has to be launched in pieces. These are then put together in space. About 45 spaceflights will be needed to launch more than 100 pieces.

International Space Station

Crew:	**3 to 7**
Length:	**108 m/356 ft**
Width:	**88 m/290 ft**
Mass when finished:	**455 tonnes**
Height above Earth:	**400 km/249 miles**

The first part of the International Space Station was launched by a Russian rocket in 1998.

The space station grows bigger as more modules (pieces) are added. This picture shows it in 2004.

Going to work in space

American Space Shuttles and Russian Soyuz spacecraft take astronauts to the ISS. They usually stay for about six months. They carry out science experiments and study the Earth.

The space station will be the biggest structure ever built in space. There will be more space inside the ISS than in the passenger cabin of a Boeing 747 Jumbo Jet.

Other space stations

The **Soviet Union** launched the first space station in 1971. It was the first of seven space stations called Salyut. The first Salyuts stayed in space for just a few months, but Salyut 7 (right) orbited Earth for nearly nine years.

Skylab

The United States launched its own space station in 1973. It was called Skylab. It was made from rockets and spacecraft that weren't needed for the Apollo moon-landing missions. Three crews visited Skylab (below).

The Salyut 7 space station was launched in 1982.

*Skylab was shaken very hard while it was being launched. This shaking caused one of its two **solar panels** to break off.*

solar panel

Mir

The Soviet Union launched its Mir space station in 1986. Then extra modules were added to it, to make it bigger. Mir stayed in space for 15 years.

Burning up

When all of these space stations reached the end of their working lives, they were left to fall into the atmosphere. As they fell, they tumbled and broke up. The smallest pieces burned up, but the biggest pieces hit the ground or fell into the sea.

Mir space station

Module	Launched	Used for
Core module	1986	control centre and living area
Kvant-1	1987	studying stars
Kvant-2	1989	spacewalks
Kristall	1990	processing materials
Spektr	1995	studying the atmosphere
Priroda	1996	studying the oceans and atmosphere

The Mir space station orbited the Earth at a height of about 390 km (242 miles).

The cleverest spacecraft

No-one has gone to other planets yet, but scientists have sent spacecraft to land on them. In 2004, two vehicles landed on Mars. They were called the Mars Exploration Rovers. One was nicknamed Spirit and the other one was called Opportunity.

1

2

3

4

5

1 Space vehicle enters atmosphere

2 Parachute pops out

3 Heat shield falls away

4 Air bags inflate

5 Rockets fire to slow the lander

6 Parachute is cut away

7 Lander bounces on air bags

8 Lander opens

9 Mars Rover is ready to go

This is how the Mars Exploration Rovers landed safely on the surface of Mars.

6

7

8

9

Looking for life

Mars is a dry, dusty planet. Scientists would like to know if it had rivers and seas in the past. If there was water on Mars, there may have been life too. There may even be some life on Mars today.

All in a day's work

The rovers study rocks. Their computers work out how to move about and do the work. When a rover reaches a rock, it uses its instruments to find out what the rock is made from.

The Mars Exploration Rovers have solar panels. These make electricity for their cameras and instruments.

radio **antenna**

cameras

camera mast

radio antenna

solar panels

Other clever spacecraft

Spirit and Opportunity weren't the first clever spacecraft to land on Mars. In 1976, two spacecraft called Viking landed on Mars. They measured the weather and they dug up some soil to test it. They also took lots of photographs of the planet's red surface. One lander worked for about 4 years. The other worked for about 6 years.

The Viking landers tested the soil on Mars, but they found no signs of life. Some scientists believe they were looking in the wrong place.

	Viking I and Viking II	Sojourner
Launched:	1975	1996
Landed on Mars:	1976	1997
Length:	3 m/9 ft 9 in	63 cm/25 in
Height:	2 m/6 ft 6 in	28 cm/11 in
Mass:	663 kg/1,462 lb	10.5 kg/23 lb

The solar panel on top of Sojourner produced electric power. This gave a top speed of about 40 centimetres (16 inches) per minute.

Driving on Mars

The Vikings couldn't move around, so in 1997 a small rover vehicle landed on Mars. It was called the Mars pathfinder rover, or Sojourner. It could go up to interesting rocks and study them with its instruments. A "driver" on Earth controlled Sojourner. Mars and Earth were so far apart that it took up to 15 minutes for commands to reach Sojourner. Sojourner kept working for nearly three months.

Scientists gave nicknames to the rocks studied by Sojourner. This rock was called "Yogi".

63 cm/25 in

The toughest spacecraft

In 1985, the European Space Agency **(ESA)** sent a spacecraft to take close-up photographs of Halley's Comet. Comets look like fuzzy smudges with long bright tails. They are chunks of rock and ice that have been flying around the Sun for billions of years.

Most spacecraft would be destroyed if they flew through the dust around a comet. ESA had to make a super-tough spacecraft for the job. The spacecraft was called Giotto.

Photographs from Giotto showed that Halley's Comet is a rock. It is about 15 kilometres (9 miles) long and 8 kilometres (5 miles) across.

Giotto flew into the dust around Halley's Comet at 249,000 kph (155,000 mph). Dust from Halley's Comet hit the Giotto spacecraft 50 times faster than a bullet!

comet dust   dust shield   solar panel   camera   dish radio antenna

Designing the dust buster

Giotto had a shield at the front to protect it from the comet's dust. The shield was made from two plates, one behind the other. Any dust that got through the front plate was caught by the plate behind it. A radio dish at the other end of the spacecraft sent photographs back to Earth.

What happened to Giotto?

Giotto was hit by dust from Halley's Comet 12,000 times, but it survived. It was then steered towards another comet, called Grigg-Skjellerup. Giotto arrived in 1992. Its camera had been destroyed by Halley's dust, but its other instruments took measurements. Then Giotto had no more fuel, so it was left to drift in space.

The most widely travelled spacecraft

In the 1970s, the outer planets moved into a line across space. This was an amazing opportunity for a spacecraft to fly past nearly all of them, one after another. In 1977, two Voyager spacecraft were sent to study these planets.

The Voyager craft

The two Voyager spacecraft carried cameras and scientific instruments. They sent thousands of pictures and lots of other information back to Earth by radio.

Each Voyager spacecraft had a large radio dish. This sent pictures and other information back to Earth.

Neptune

cameras and other instruments

radio antenna

nuclear electricity generator

radio dish

radio antenna

Still going

Both Voyagers are now heading out of the **solar system** towards the stars. They should keep working until about 2020. But which of them has travelled the furthest? The answer is Voyager 1. It is now about 14.4 billion kilometres (about 9 billion miles) away.

The Voyagers' Grand Tour

	Voyager 1	Voyager 2
Launched:	1977	1977
Jupiter:	1979	1979
Saturn:	1980	1981
Uranus:	–	1986
Neptune:	–	1989

Voyagers 1 and 2 took different paths through the solar system. Voyager 1 flew past Jupiter and Saturn. Voyager 2's flight path took it past four planets!

Each Voyager spacecraft was quite big – the dish alone was 3.7 metres (12 feet 1 inch) across.

7.5 m/24 ft 7 in

Sun

Earth
93,000,000 miles from sun

The distance from the Earth to the Sun is 93,000,000 miles. Follow the arrows to find out how far Voyager 1 has flown.

Facts and figures

There have been dozens of space vehicles. Some of them are listed here. You can use the information to see which are the biggest and heaviest, which have made the most flights, which were built first and how many people they carried. Some rockets are made in lots of different versions. These are used for launching different spacecraft. Some of the figures change from mission to mission. If you want to know more about these or other space vehicles, look on pages 30 and 31 to find out how to do some research.

One-person space capsules	Height	Base width	Mass	Manned missions
Mercury (USA)	2.9 m/9.6 ft	1.9 m/6.2 ft	1,935 kg/4,265 lb	6 (1961–1963)
Vostok (USSR)	2.3 m/7 ft 7 in	2.3 m/7 ft 7 in	2,460 kg/5,423 lb	6 (1961–1963)

Two-person space capsules	Height	Base width	Mass	Manned missions
Gemini (USA)	5.6 m/18 ft 5 in	3.1 m/10 ft	3,760 kg/8,290 lb	10 (1965–1966)

Three-person spacecraft	Height	Base width	Mass	Manned missions
Apollo Command Module (USA)	3.2 m/10 ft 7 in	3.9 m/12 ft 10 in	29,600 kg/65,225 lb	15 (1968–1975)
Shenzhou (China)	8.65 m/28 ft 5 in	2.8 m/9 ft 2 in	7,800 kg/17,200 lb	1 (2003)
Soyuz (Russia)	7.0 m/23 ft	2.7 m/9 ft	7,220 kg/15,915 lb	more than 90*

* The Soyuz TMA spacecraft is still being used.

Spaceplanes	Length	Wingspan	Take-off weight	Number built
Buran (USSR)	36.37 m/119 ft 4 in	23.92 m/78 ft 6 in	75,000 kg/165,000 lb	1
Space Shuttle (USA)	37.2 m/122 ft	23.8 m/78 ft	99,318 kg/218,960 lb	6*

* including an Orbiter called Enterprise that has not gone into space

Space Stations	Launched	Mass	Time in space	Fell back to Earth
Skylab (USA)	1973	76.3 tonnes	6 years	1979
Salyut 7 (USSR)	1982	18.9 tonnes	9 years	1991
Mir (USSR)	1986	135 tonnes	15 years	2001
International Space Station	1998	455 tonnes	Still being built	Still in space

Satellites and space probes	Launched	Length or diameter*	Mass	Planets visited
Sputnik 1 (USSR)	1957	58 cm/23 in	84 kg/185 lb	Orbited Earth
Mariner 9 (USA)	1971	5.6 m/18 ft 4 in	1,031 kg/2,273 lb	Orbited Mars
Pioneer 11 (USA)	1973	2.7 m/8 ft 10 in	270 kg/595 lb	Flew past Jupiter and Saturn
Voyager 2 (USA)	1977	3.7 m/12 ft 2 in	825 kg/1,819 lb	Flew past Jupiter, Saturn, Uranus, and Neptune
Magellan (USA)	1989	6.4 m/21 ft	3,444 kg/7,593 lb	Orbited Venus
Galileo (USA)	1989	9.0 m/29 ft 6 in	3,881 kg/8,556 lb	Orbited Jupiter

* Satellites and space probes are different shapes, so it is difficult to give their sizes. These figures give an approximate comparison.

Landers	Launched	Length/diameter	Mass	Landed
Luna 9 (USSR)	1966	60 cm/24 in	100 kg/220 lb	Moon, 1966
Venera 9 (USSR)	1975	2.4 m/7 ft 11 in	1,560 kg/3,440 lb	Venus, 1975
Viking 1 & 2 (USA)	1975	3 m/9 ft 9 in	663 kg/1,462 lb	Mars, 1976
Sojourner (USA)	1996	63 cm/2ft 1 in	10.5 kg/23 lb	Mars, 1997
Huygens (Europe)	1997	2.7 m/8 ft 10 in	318 kg/700 lb	Titan (a moon of Saturn), 2005
Mars Exploration Rovers (USA)	2003	1.6 m/5 ft 3 in	185 kg/408 lb	Mars, 2004

Rockets	When used	Height	Mass	Used to launch
Vostok (USSR)	1960–1964	30.8 m/101 ft	281,375 kg/620,325 lb	Vostok spacecraft
Redstone-Mercury (USA)	1961	25.3 m/83 ft	29,935 kg/66,000 lb	Early Mercury spacecraft
Atlas-Mercury (USA)	1962–1963	28.3 m/92 ft 10 in	166,460 kg/366,985 lb	Later Mercury spacecraft
Titan-Gemini (USA)	1964–1966	33.2 m/108 ft 11 in	148,325 kg/327,000 lb	Gemini spacecraft
Saturn V (USA)	1967–1972	111 m/364 ft 2 in	2,938,312 kg/6,477,900 lb	Apollo moon-landing spacecraft
Soyuz (USSR)	1966–today	46.1 m/151 ft 3 in	305,000 kg/672,410 lb	Soyuz spacecraft
Proton (Russia)	1965–today	50.0 m/164 ft	693,810 kg/1,529,590 lb	Space Station parts and satellites
Energia-Buran (Russia)	1988	97.0 m/318 ft3 in	2,524,600 kg/5,565,810 lb	Buran spaceplane
Ariane 5 (Europe)	2002–today	55.4 m/181ft 9 in	750,000 kg/1,653,470 lb	Satellites

Glossary

antenna part of a radio that sends or receives radio waves. Radio antennae sometimes have metal dishes. These collect more radio waves or send them out in a stronger beam. Aerial is another word for antenna.

astronaut American or European space traveller. Russian space travellers are called cosmonauts.

atmosphere the air or other gases around a planet

Command Module control centre and living area of the Apollo spacecraft

cosmonaut Russian space traveller

ESA European Space Agency. It is the organisation that manages non-military spaceflights for Europe.

Lunar Excursion Module (LEM) part of the Apollo spacecraft. It carried astronauts from orbit around the Moon down to the Moon's surface.

mission a task carried out by one or more astronauts or robot craft during a spaceflight

module part of a spacecraft, for example the Apollo spacecraft's Command Module

nuclear electricity generator device used by spacecraft to make electricity. It works by changing heat produced naturally by materials like uranium and plutonium into electricity.

orbit path of a spacecraft around a planet or moon. Also, the path of a moon around a planet, or a planet around the Sun.

payload equipment, astronauts, or satellites carried by a spacecraft

Service Module part of the Apollo spacecraft. It supplied the Command Module with water, electricity, gases, and rocket power.

solar panel sheet of solar cells on a spacecraft. These change sunlight into electricity. Spacecraft need electricity to power their cameras, instruments, and radio equipment.

solar system the Sun and everything that circles it – the nine planets, their moons, and all the other pieces of rock and ice that fly around the Sun

Soviet Union the group of countries led by Russia that launched the first satellite, the first manned spacecraft, and the first space station. Also known as the USSR.

space probe an unmanned spacecraft used to explore space

thruster small rocket or gas-jet that is fired to make small changes to a spacecraft's position

Voyager 1 has travelled 9,000,000,000 miles!

Voyager 1 9,000,000,000 miles

Finding out more

You can find out more by looking for other books to read and searching the internet.

Books
Here are some more books about space, spaceflight, and space vehicles:

e.explore – Space Travel, by Ian Graham (Dorling Kindersley, 2004)

How Science Works – Rockets and Other Spacecraft, by John Farndon (Franklin Watts, 2003)

Monster Machines – Spacecraft, by David Jefferis (Belitha Press, 2002)

Space vehicles online
These web sites give more information about space vehicles:

http://kids.msfc.nasa.gov/ – this web site has lots of information about the American space agency NASA.

http://esamultimedia.esa.int/multimedia/gamekids/esa-en/index.html – this is the offical web site of ESA, the European Space Agency.

More to do
You can find plans to make your own model Mars Pathfinder spacecraft at:
http://mars.jpl.nasa.gov/MPF/mpf/education/cutouts.html

Space vehicles of the past
How do today's space vehicles compare to the space vehicles of past times? You can find out about old space vehicles at:
http://science.howstuffworks.com/project-mercury.htm

Can you find out what was carried inside the second satellite ever launched, Sputnik 2? Was it:
1 A dog?
2 Nothing – it was empty?
3 A tape recorder playing music?
(Answer on page 32.)

You can also find information about record-breaking spacecraft and spaceflights at:
http://guinnessworldrecords.com

Index

Answer to question on page 31

A dog. On 3 November 1957, Sputnik 2 was launched into space. It had a dog called Laika inside. Laika was the first living creature to orbit the Earth.

Titles in the *The World's Greatest...* series include:

Hardback   1-844-21262-9

Hardback   1-844-21263-7

Hardback   1-844-21264-5

Hardback   1-844-21265-3

Hardback   1-844-21266-1

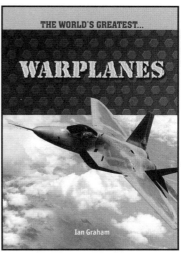

Hardback   1-844-21267-X

Find out about other titles from Raintree on our website www.raintreepublishers.co.uk